The 25th Amendment

We All Fall Down

By J. G. Taylor

J. G. Taylor

J. G. Taylor

This book is dedicated to:

The lone voter, who must have a voice

J. G. Taylor

Forward:

History is a character, all its own, a non-fiction character but a character never the less. While doing some research on another idea I came across The 25th Amendment. I hadn't thought about it in a number of years. In fact it was completely gone to the adult me. It came back to me from a long ago place and time.

After reading it I now have an idea what it could mean to us in this current century. Or actually at any time since it was ratified.

My hope is that you will read what I've compiled here and make a just and good decision on what this Amendment and our Constitution represents to every citizen of our own small planet, not just American citizens.

I am not advocating the use of said Amendment or against the use of said Amendment. I am just trying to present the facts as they have been presented to us by history and by law. And by my own memory.

I have inserted the Amendments that were ratified before and after the 25ᵗʰ Amendment to give a feel for the history of the Amendments and the times they were ratified.

I have also inserted the entire United States Constitution.

My greatest hope is that you will read the entire Constitution of the United States of America.

J. G. Taylor

On each reading I'm inspired by the great men and woman who brought The United States of America to reality.

This is not an attempt to influence any one. It is rather meant to inform and enlighten.

My fear in the face of all the happenings in our world is that the vision of our great and forward thinking forbearers has not and will not be lost to us as a people or to the person whom I have dedicated this book- the one lone voter.

It's your right as given to us by our forbearers!

You have the voice.

You have the power.

I usually parallel all thoughts on the rights given to the people who live within the confines of the United States of American to that of a parent and a child/children.

Further my thoughts- every parent should spend their days protecting their child/children and trying to guide the same through to adulthood. With the hopes they will become a productive member of society.

Our forebears attempted to do the same with our Constitution along with the Bill of Rights and the various Amendments as the protection and guides for the new country they were creating, their child in essence.

J. G. Taylor

In the long history of our planet, I equate the current time for the United States of America as the early part of adolescences'.

As any parent of a grown child will tell you the success or failure of said child can be almost directly related to early adolescence.

The checks and balances of United States Government are the three branches of this government, they would be what kept the child in order, and these would be the disciplines.

Therefore also included are several pages dedicated to explaining the three parts of United States government. Where the rules, the curfew, the chores, are put into place- the laws.

Chapter 1

The Amendment before:

The 24th Amendent

We lived in a little house on 53rd street in Lubbock Texas in 1963 and 1964. I was 5 years old in 1963 and early 1964. As I sat under my mother's ironing board playing with blocks I had no idea the world was changed forever by Mr. Trout fifteen years before I was even born.

I just remember my father sitting at the table while my mother ironed and they talked about the happenings of the government and of the world. My father was a kitchen table politician.

J. G. Taylor

He spent a lot of time telling my mother exactly what we should be doing. Looking at his assessments from memories door more often than not he was correct.

The 24th Amendent was ratified just weeks after an event which would lead up to the 25th Amendent, the assignation of President John F. Kennedy.

Oddly, in that earlier time that November day in 1963 I was under the same ironing board playing with the same blocks listening to my parents talk about what had just happened in Dallas. My mother was crying.

Back to the 24th Amendment.

About and the history of the 24th Amendent:

It was more than twenty years after Atlanta textile worker Mr. Trout complained about his not being able to vote to a WPA interviewer, collection of poll taxes in national elections was prohibited by the January 23, 1964, ratification of the Twenty-Fourth Amendment to the Constitution.

Passage of the amendment changed voting in Alabama, Mississippi, Arkansas, Texas, and Virginia.

Source: Library of Congress

Amendment XXIV (the Twenty-fourth Amendment) prohibits both Congress and the states from conditioning the right to vote in federal elections on payment of a poll tax or other types of tax. The amendment was proposed by Congress to the states on August 27, 1962, and was ratified by the states on January 23, 1964.

J. G. Taylor

Poll taxes had been enacted in 11 Southern states after Reconstruction as a measure to prevent African Americans from voting, and had been held to be unconstitutional by the United States Supreme Court. At the time of this amendment's passage, only five states still retained a poll tax: Virginia, Alabama, Texas, Arkansas, and Mississippi. However, it wasn't until the U.S. Supreme Court ruled 6-3 in Harper v. Virginia Board of Elections (1966) that all state poll taxes (for both state and federal elections) were officially declared unconstitutional, because they violated the Equal Protection Clause of the Fourteenth Amendment.

Source: Wikipedia

"Do you know I've never voted in my life, never been able to exercise my right as a citizen because of the poll tax?"

Mr. Trout

Amendment XXIV

Section 1.

The right of citizens of the United States to vote in any primary or other election for President or Vice President, for electors for President or Vice President, or for Senator or Representative in Congress, shall not be denied or abridged by the United States or any state by reason of failure to pay any poll tax or other tax.

J. G. Taylor

Section 2.

The Congress shall have power to enforce this article by appropriate legislation.

Chapter 2

The Amendment after:

We had moved across the Nation to the Northwest by the time The 26ᵗʰ Amendent came in to being. It was the time of continued unrest in The United States of America over an unwanted war. This unwanted war was about to end badly in the first true loss in a war for the United States of America.

I remember sitting on the sofa while my father applauded the TV news anchor talking about the ratification of the 26ᵗʰ Amendent. My father a former United States Marine said, "About damn time. If you're old enough to fight you should be able to say who it was that put you there." He wasn't talking to me in particular more to the TV and the time.

For me the only person whom I had ever known who was sent to war while I watched and who didn't have the right to vote was our strawberry picking bus's 18 year old driver. His number came up in the lottery two years before this Amendent was ratified and he was sent to Vietnam.

I didn't see him again until a couple years later, after the 26th Amendment was ratified. We were sitting in a pizza parlor. Four years later he was no longer the tanned vibrate youth of my young childhood but walked with a cane and a limp. I didn't ask but I assumed and I assume to this day he was injured in the war. A war where he had no voice, no choice, no vote.

The 26th Amendment:

About and the history:

During World War II, President Franklin D. Roosevelt lowered the minimum age for the draft to 18, at a time when the minimum voting age (as determined by the individual states) had historically been 21. "Old enough to fight, old enough to vote" became a common slogan for a youth voting rights movement, and in 1943 Georgia became the first state to lower its voting age in state and local elections from 21 to 18.

Jennings Randolph, then a Democratic congressman from West Virginia, introduced federal legislation to lower the voting age in 1942; it was the first of 11 times that Randolph, who was later elected to the Senate, would introduce such a bill in

J. G. Taylor

Congress. The driving force behind Randolph's efforts was his faith in America's youth, of whom he believed: "They possess a great social conscience, are perplexed by the injustices in the world and are anxious to rectify those ills."

Presidential & Congressional Support for the 26th Amendment

Dwight D. Eisenhower, who led the U.S. armed forces to victory in Europe in 1945, later became the first president to publicly voice his support for a constitutional amendment lowering the minimum voting age. In his 1954 State of the Union address.

Eisenhower declared: "For years our citizens between the ages of 18 and 21 have, in time of peril, been summoned to fight for America. They should participate in the political process that produces this fateful summons."

In the late 1960s, with the United States embroiled in a long, costly war in Vietnam, youth voting rights activists held marches and demonstrations to draw lawmakers' attention to the hypocrisy of drafting young men and women who lacked the right to vote. In 1969, no fewer than 60 resolutions were introduced in Congress to lower the minimum voting age, but none resulted in any action. The following year, when Congress passed a bill extending and amending the Voting Rights Act of 1965, it contained a provision that lowered the voting age to 18 in federal, state and local elections. Though he signed the bill into law, President Richard M. Nixon issued a public statement declaring that he believed the provision to be unconstitutional.

J. G. Taylor

"Although I strongly favor the 18-year-old vote," Nixon continued, "I believe–along with most of the Nation's leading constitutional scholars–that Congress has no power to enact it by simple statute, but rather it requires a constitutional amendment.

Supreme Court Decision on the 26th Amendment

In the 1970 case Oregon v. Mitchell, the U.S. Supreme Court was tasked with reviewing the constitutionality of the provision. Justice Hugo Black wrote the majority decision in the case, which held that Congress did not have the right to regulate the minimum age in State and local elections, but only in federal elections.

The issue left the Court divided: Four justices, not including Black, believed Congress did have the right in state and local elections, while four others (again, not including Black) believed that Congress lacked the right even for federal elections, and that under the Constitution only the states have the right to set voter qualifications.

Under this verdict, 18- to 20-year-olds would be eligible to vote for president and vice president, but not for state officials up for election at the same time. Dissatisfaction with this situation—as well as public reaction to the protests of large numbers of young men and women facing conscription, but deprived of the right to vote—built support among many states for a Constitutional amendment that would set a uniform national voting age of 18 in all elections.

J. G. Taylor

Passage, Ratification and Effects of the 26th Amendment

On March 10, 1971, the U.S. Senate voted unanimously in favor of the proposed amendment. After an overwhelming House vote in favor on March 23, the 26th Amendment went to the states for ratification. In just over two months–the shortest period of time for any amendment in U.S. history–the necessary three-fourths of state legislatures (or 38 states) ratified the 26th Amendment, and President Nixon signed it into law that July.

At a White House ceremony attended by 500 newly eligible voters, Nixon declared: "The reason I believe that your generation, the 11 million new voters, will do so much for America at home is that you will infuse into this nation some idealism, some courage, some stamina, some high moral purpose, that this country always needs."

Though newly minted young voters were expected to choose Democratic challenger George McGovern, an opponent of the Vietnam War, Nixon was reelected by an overwhelming margin–winning 49 states– in 1972. Over the next decades, the legacy of the 26th Amendment was a mixed one: After a 55.4 percent turnout in 1972, youth turnout steadily declined, reaching 36 percent in the 1988 presidential election.

Though the 1992 election of Bill Clinton saw a slight rebound, voting rates of 18- to 24-year-olds remained well behind the turnout of older voters, and many lamented that America's young people were squandering their opportunities to enact change.

J. G. Taylor

The 2008 presidential election of Barack Obama saw a voter turnout of some 49 percent of 18- to 24 year-olds, the second highest in history.

Source: The History Channel

The presidential election of 2016 has yet to be determined.

Amendment XXVI

Section 1.

The right of citizens of the United States, who are 18 years of age or older, to vote, shall not be denied or abridged by the United States or any state on account of age.

Section 2.

The Congress shall have the power to enforce this article by appropriate legislation.

J. G. Taylor

Chapter 3

Now we have come to the so called meat and potatoes of this compilation. This books namesake- *The 25th Amendent.*

1967 the year *The 25th Amendent* was ratified is in my humble opinion one of the pivotal times in the history of the United States of America. I am not alone in my pivotal assessment of 1967.

It was ratified only months from the *Summer of Love* and in my own case from the summer of my first true love a little Pinto colt.

San Francisco's Haight Ashbury, Hippies, the first heart transplant, the first

Super Bowl, and much more were all part of 1967.

It was just a little over a year before two more of our great leaders would be needlessly lost to us as a country. "I have a dream," wouldn't be lost just changed. In fact the whole world was changing, along with the rights of the citizens of the United States of America.

The 25ᵗʰ Amendment

The Twenty-fifth Amendment of the United States Constitution gives a concise outline of the succession to the Presidency and establishes practices for filling a vacancy in the office of the Vice President or for a Presidential incapacity.

J. G. Taylor

This Amendment replaces the unclear wording of Article II- Section 1- Clause 6 of the Constitution, which does not clarify if the Vice President becomes the President or Acting President if the President dies, resigns, is removed from office, or is otherwise unable to discharge the powers or the duties of the presidency.

The 25th Amendment was adopted on February 10, 1967.

The 25th Amendment:

Amendment XXV

Section 1.

In case of the removal of the President from office or of his death or resignation, the Vice President shall become President.

Section 2.

Whenever there is a vacancy in the office of the Vice President, the President shall nominate a Vice President who shall take office upon confirmation by a majority vote of both Houses of Congress.

Section 3.

Whenever the President transmits to the President pro tempore of the Senate and the Speaker of the House of Representatives his written declaration that he is unable to discharge the powers and duties of his office, and until he transmits to them a written declaration to the contrary, such powers and duties shall be discharged by the Vice President as Acting President.

Section 4.

Whenever the Vice President and a majority of either the principal officers of the

J. G. Taylor

executive departments or of such other body as Congress may by law provide, transmit to the President pro tempore of the Senate and the Speaker of the House of Representatives their written declaration that the President is unable to discharge the powers and duties of his office, the Vice President shall immediately assume the powers and duties of the office as Acting President.

Thereafter, when the President transmits to the President pro tempore of the Senate and the Speaker of the House of Representatives his written declaration that no inability exists, he shall resume the powers and duties of his office unless the Vice President and a majority of either the principal officers of the executive department or of such other body as Congress may by law provide, transmit within four days to the President pro tempore of the Senate and the

Speaker of the House of Representatives their written declaration that the President is unable to discharge the powers and duties of his office.

Thereupon Congress shall decide the issue, assembling within forty-eight hours for that If the Congress, within twenty-one days after receipt of the latter written declaration, or, if Congress is not in session, within twenty-one days after Congress is required to assemble, determines by two-thirds vote of both Houses that the President is unable to discharge the powers and duties of his office, the Vice President shall continue to discharge the same as Acting President; otherwise, the President shall resume the powers and duties of his office.

J. G. Taylor

Chapter 4

History of the 25th Amendment

Source: History News Network

The 25th Amendment provides two remedies when a president is disabled. 1. The president of his own volition may turn over the power of his office to the vice president. 2. The vice president, with the assent of a majority of the leading members of the cabinet, may make himself acting president on a temporary basis.

The disability clause of the amendment has never been formally invoked until now.

Wire Service reports indicate that White House Counsel Al Gonzales has expressly

indicated that the president plans to invoke the amendment.

In July 1985 President Ronald Reagan underwent an operation to remove a cancerous tissue from his colon.

In anticipation of his operation, which required him to be anesthetized,

President Reagan sent a letter to the speaker of the House of Representatives and to the president pro tem of the Senate notifying them that he was turning over the powers of the presidency to Vice President George Herbert Walker Bush:

"I have determined and it is my intention and direction that Vice President George Bush shall discharge powers and duties in my stead, commencing with the administration of anesthesia to me.

J. G. Taylor

" This is the procedure outlined in the 25th Amendment, but President Reagan expressly indicated that he was not invoking the amendment.

"I do not believe," he wrote in his letter to the Congress.

"In that the drafters of this amendment intended its application to situations such as the present one." Various explanations have been offered for what one scholar, Thomas Cronin, refers to as this "curious sentence." Cronin has suggested Reagan "and his aides feared that Reagan might have further illnesses and operations and that frequent invoking of this section [of the 25th Amendment] might diminish Reagan's leadership image.

"But it is also possible that Reagan was attempting to avoid setting a precedent that might bind his successors (or himself). Eight hours after he gave up power he signed a second letter taking it back.

Controversy Involving the Disability Clause.

In 1981, after being shot by John Hinkley, President Reagan was rushed to the hospital and nearly died from blood loss. The president did not invoke the 25th Amendment, though his aides intensively debated whether he should.

In the White House, Secretary of State Alexander Haig famously claimed that he "was in charge" pending the return of Vice President Bush. In fact, in the event of a national security emergency, the vice president and the secretary of defense were

J. G. Taylor

"clearly entrusted by Reagan to act in his absence."

According to the latest edition of Edward S. Corwin's magisterial book, The President.

In 1985 President Reagan again did not invoke the 25th Amendment, but he did at least seem to honor the intent of the law by notifying the leaders of Congress by letter that he was turning power over to the vice president.

That a president can turn over his power without formally invoking the amendment is unclear and has never been tested in court. Oddly, Vice President Bush was not immediately informed about the letter giving him the power of the presidency.

Eight hours after Mr. Reagan signed the letter he took back the power of the presidency by signing a second letter given to him by White House Chief of Staff Donald Regan. The president was still groggy from the anesthesia and barely managed to scribble his name.

General John Hutton, the presidential physician, afterward told the New York Times that the president signed the letter without his knowledge.

"I would have waited at least a day," Hutton said.

"I don't know why his chief of staff insisted on him signing the letter so quickly." (NYT, Dec. 4, 1996).

J. G. Taylor

President George Herbert Walker Bush fell seriously ill twice during his presidency. On neither occasion did he invoke the 25th Amendment. But in 1991, when he suffered from an irregular heartbeat, he announced that if he needed electric shock therapy he would temporarily turn power over to Vice President Dan Quayle.

President Clinton never fell seriously ill during his presidency.

Both Presidents George Herbert Walker Bush and Clinton made arrangements with their vice presidents in the event of illness. These contingency plans were never invoked and remain secret.

In 1996 a panel of historians and former White House physicians issued a formal report recommending urgent changes in the way presidential power is transferred in the event of disability.

These changes, which the panel recommended should be put into law, included:

(1) A formal requirement that the president and vice president agree on a transfer-of-power contingency plan prior to their inauguration:

(2)the president's personal physician should make primary judgments about the president's health;

(3) the White House physician, who by tradition was a member of the White House Military Office, should be given a formal title outside the chain of military command (for example: assistant to the president);

J. G. Taylor

(4) the judgment of the president's physical abilities should be determined strictly on the basis of standard medical tests, and (5) presidents should accurately disclose their medical condition, balancing their need for privacy against the public's need for information.

Background to the 25th Amendment

Source: findlaw.com

"The Twenty-fifth Amendment was an effort to resolve some of the continuing issues revolving about the office of the President; that is, what happens upon the death, removal, or resignation of the President and what is the course to follow if for some reason the President becomes disabled to such a

degree that he cannot fulfill his
responsibilities?

The practice had been well established
that the Vice President became President
upon the death of the President, as had
happened eight times in our history.
Presumably, the Vice President would
become President upon the removal of the
President from office.

Whether the Vice President would
become acting President when the President
became unable to carry on and whether the
President could resume his office upon his
recovering his ability were two questions that
had divided scholars and experts.

Also, seven Vice Presidents had died in
office and one had resigned, so that for some

J. G. Taylor

twenty per cent of United States history there had been no Vice President to step up. But the seemingly most insoluble problem was that of presidential inability--Garfield lying in a coma for eighty days before succumbing to the effects of an assassin's bullet.

Wilson an invalid for the last eighteen months of his term, the result of a stroke--with its unanswered questions: who was to determine the existence of an inability, how was the matter to be handled if the President sought to continue, in what manner should the Vice President act, would he be acting President or President, what was to happen if the President recovered.

Congress finally proposed this Amendment to the States in the aftermath of President Kennedy's assassination, with the

Vice Presidency vacant and a President who had previously had a heart attack.

"This Amendment saw multiple use during the 1970s and resulted for the first time in our history in the accession to the Presidency and Vice-Presidency of two men who had not faced the voters in a national election.

First, Vice President Spiro Agnew resigned on October 10, 1973, and President Nixon nominated Gerald R. Ford of Michigan to succeed him, following the procedures of Sec. 2 of the Amendment for the first time. Hearings were held upon the nomination by the Senate Rules Committee and the House Judiciary Committee, both Houses thereafter confirmed the nomination, and the new Vice President took the oath of office December 6, 1973.

J. G. Taylor

Second, President Richard M. Nixon resigned his office August 9, 1974, and Vice President Ford immediately succeeded to the office and took the presidential oath of office at noon of the same day. Third, again following Sec. 2 of the Amendment, President Ford nominated Nelson A. Rockefeller of New York to be Vice President; on August 20, 1974, hearings were held in both Houses, confirmation voted and Mr. Rockefeller took the oath of office December 19, 1974.[1]"

Chapter 5

The Constitution

Below is the United States Constitution. I have read this most important of documents many times. My hope is that you will read it now.

The Constitution of the United States: A Transcription

Note: The following text is a transcription of the Constitution as it was inscribed by Jacob Shallus on parchment (the document on display in the Rotunda at the National Archives Museum.) The spelling and punctuation reflects the original.

J. G. Taylor

We the People of the United States, in Order to form a more perfect Union, establish Justice, insure domestic Tranquility, provide for the common defence, promote the general Welfare, and secure the Blessings of Liberty to ourselves and our Posterity, do ordain and establish this Constitution for the United States of America.

Article. I.

Section. 1.

All legislative Powers herein granted shall be vested in a Congress of the United States, which shall consist of a Senate and House of Representatives.

Section. 2.

The House of Representatives shall be composed of Members chosen every second Year by the People of the several States, and

the Electors in each State shall have the Qualifications requisite for Electors of the most numerous Branch of the State Legislature.

No Person shall be a Representative who shall not have attained to the Age of twenty five Years, and been seven Years a Citizen of the United States, and who shall not, when elected, be an Inhabitant of that State in which he shall be chosen.

Representatives and direct Taxes shall be apportioned among the several States which may be included within this Union, according to their respective Numbers, which shall be determined by adding to the whole Number of free Persons, including those bound to Service for a Term of Years, and excluding Indians not taxed, three fifths of all other Persons. The actual Enumeration shall be made within three Years after the first Meeting of the Congress of the United States,

J. G. Taylor

and within every subsequent Term of ten Years, in such Manner as they shall by Law direct.

The Number of Representatives shall not exceed one for every thirty Thousand, but each State shall have at Least one Representative; and until such enumeration shall be made, the State of New Hampshire shall be entitled to chuse three, Massachusetts eight, Rhode-Island and Providence Plantations one, Connecticut five, New-York six, New Jersey four, Pennsylvania eight, Delaware one, Maryland six, Virginia ten, North Carolina five, South Carolina five, and Georgia three.

When vacancies happen in the Representation from any State, the Executive Authority thereof shall issue Writs of Election to fill such Vacancies.

The House of Representatives shall chuse their Speaker and other Officers; and shall have the sole Power of Impeachment.

Section. 3.

The Senate of the United States shall be composed of two Senators from each State, chosen by the Legislature thereof, for six Years; and each Senator shall have one Vote.

Immediately after they shall be assembled in Consequence of the first Election, they shall be divided as equally as may be into three Classes. The Seats of the Senators of the first Class shall be vacated at the Expiration of the second Year, of the second Class at the Expiration of the fourth Year, and of the third Class at the Expiration of the sixth Year, so that one third may be chosen every second Year; and if Vacancies happen by Resignation, or otherwise, during the Recess

J. G. Taylor

of the Legislature of any State, the Executive thereof may make temporary Appointments until the next Meeting of the Legislature, which shall then fill such Vacancies.

No Person shall be a Senator who shall not have attained to the Age of thirty Years, and been nine Years a Citizen of the United States, and who shall not, when elected, be an Inhabitant of that State for which he shall be chosen.

The Vice President of the United States shall be President of the Senate, but shall have no Vote, unless they be equally divided.

The Senate shall chuse their other Officers, and also a President pro tempore, in the Absence of the Vice President, or when he shall exercise the Office of President of the United States.

The Senate shall have the sole Power to try all Impeachments. When sitting for that

Purpose, they shall be on Oath or Affirmation. When the President of the United States is tried, the Chief Justice shall preside: And no Person shall be convicted without the Concurrence of two thirds of the Members present.

Judgment in Cases of Impeachment shall not extend further than to removal from Office, and disqualification to hold and enjoy any Office of honor, Trust or Profit under the United States: but the Party convicted shall nevertheless be liable and subject to Indictment, Trial, Judgment and Punishment, according to Law.

Section. 4.

The Times, Places and Manner of holding Elections for Senators and Representatives, shall be prescribed in each State by the Legislature thereof; but the Congress may at any time by Law make or alter such

J. G. Taylor

Regulations, except as to the Places of chusing Senators.

The Congress shall assemble at least once in every Year, and such Meeting shall be on the first Monday in December, unless they shall by Law appoint a different Day.

Section. 5.

Each House shall be the Judge of the Elections, Returns and Qualifications of its own Members, and a Majority of each shall constitute a Quorum to do Business; but a smaller Number may adjourn from day to day, and may be authorized to compel the Attendance of absent Members, in such Manner, and under such Penalties as each House may provide.

Each House may determine the Rules of its Proceedings, punish its Members for disorderly Behaviour, and, with the Concurrence of two thirds, expel a Member.

Each House shall keep a Journal of its Proceedings, and from time to time publish the same, excepting such Parts as may in their Judgment require Secrecy; and the Yeas and Nays of the Members of either House on any question shall, at the Desire of one fifth of those Present, be entered on the Journal.

Neither House, during the Session of Congress, shall, without the Consent of the other, adjourn for more than three days, nor to any other Place than that in which the two Houses shall be sitting.

Section. 6.

The Senators and Representatives shall receive a Compensation for their Services, to be ascertained by Law, and paid out of the Treasury of the United States. They shall in

J. G. Taylor

all Cases, except Treason, Felony and Breach of the Peace, be privileged from Arrest during their Attendance at the Session of their respective Houses, and in going to and returning from the same; and for any Speech or Debate in either House, they shall not be questioned in any other Place.

No Senator or Representative shall, during the Time for which he was elected, be appointed to any civil Office under the Authority of the United States, which shall have been created, or the Emoluments whereof shall have been encreased during such time; and no Person holding any Office under the United States, shall be a Member of either House during his Continuance in Office.

Section. 7.

All Bills for raising Revenue shall originate in the House of Representatives; but the Senate may propose or concur with Amendments as on other Bills.

Every Bill which shall have passed the House of Representatives and the Senate, shall, before it become a Law, be presented to the President of the United States; If he approve he shall sign it, but if not he shall return it, with his Objections to that House in which it shall have originated, who shall enter the Objections at large on their Journal, and proceed to reconsider it. If after such Reconsideration two thirds of that House shall agree to pass the Bill, it shall be sent, together with the Objections, to the other House, by which it shall likewise be reconsidered, and if approved by two thirds of that House, it shall become a Law. But in all such Cases the Votes of both Houses shall be determined by yeas and Nays, and the Names of the Persons voting for and against the Bill shall be entered on the Journal of

J. G. Taylor

each House respectively. If any Bill shall not be returned by the President within ten Days (Sundays excepted) after it shall have been presented to him, the Same shall be a Law, in like Manner as if he had signed it, unless the Congress by their Adjournment prevent its Return, in which Case it shall not be a Law.

Every Order, Resolution, or Vote to which the Concurrence of the Senate and House of Representatives may be necessary (except on a question of Adjournment) shall be presented to the President of the United States; and before the Same shall take Effect, shall be approved by him, or being disapproved by him, shall be repassed by two thirds of the Senate and House of Representatives, according to the Rules and Limitations prescribed in the Case of a Bill.

Section. 8.

The Congress shall have Power To lay and collect Taxes, Duties, Imposts and Excises, to pay the Debts and provide for the common Defence and general Welfare of the United States; but all Duties, Imposts and Excises shall be uniform throughout the United States;

To borrow Money on the credit of the United States;

To regulate Commerce with foreign Nations, and among the several States, and with the Indian Tribes;

To establish an uniform Rule of Naturalization, and uniform Laws on the subject of Bankruptcies throughout the United States;

To coin Money, regulate the Value thereof, and of foreign Coin, and fix the Standard of Weights and Measures;

J. G. Taylor

To provide for the Punishment of counterfeiting the Securities and current Coin of the United States;

To establish Post Offices and post Roads;

To promote the Progress of Science and useful Arts, by securing for limited Times to Authors and Inventors the exclusive Right to their respective Writings and Discoveries;

To constitute Tribunals inferior to the supreme Court;

To define and punish Piracies and Felonies committed on the high Seas, and Offences against the Law of Nations;

To declare War, grant Letters of Marque and Reprisal, and make Rules concerning Captures on Land and Water;

To raise and support Armies, but no Appropriation of Money to that Use shall be for a longer Term than two Years;

To provide and maintain a Navy;

To make Rules for the Government and Regulation of the land and naval Forces;

To provide for calling forth the Militia to execute the Laws of the Union, suppress Insurrections and repel Invasions;

To provide for organizing, arming, and disciplining, the Militia, and for governing such Part of them as may be employed in the Service of the United States, reserving to the States respectively, the Appointment of the Officers, and the Authority of training the Militia according to the discipline prescribed by Congress;

To exercise exclusive Legislation in all Cases whatsoever, over such District (not exceeding ten Miles square) as may, by Cession of particular States, and the Acceptance of Congress, become the Seat of the Government of the United States, and to

J. G. Taylor

exercise like Authority over all Places purchased by the Consent of the Legislature of the State in which the Same shall be, for the Erection of Forts, Magazines, Arsenals, dock-Yards, and other needful Buildings;— And

To make all Laws which shall be necessary and proper for carrying into Execution the foregoing Powers, and all other Powers vested by this Constitution in the Government of the United States, or in any Department or Officer thereof.

Section. 9.

The Migration or Importation of such Persons as any of the States now existing shall think proper to admit, shall not be prohibited by the Congress prior to the Year one thousand eight hundred and eight, but a Tax or duty may be imposed on such

Importation, not exceeding ten dollars for each Person.

The Privilege of the Writ of Habeas Corpus shall not be suspended, unless when in Cases of Rebellion or Invasion the public Safety may require it.

No Bill of Attainder or ex post facto Law shall be passed.

No Capitation, or other direct, Tax shall be laid, unless in Proportion to the Census or enumeration herein before directed to be taken.

No Tax or Duty shall be laid on Articles exported from any State.

No Preference shall be given by any Regulation of Commerce or Revenue to the Ports of one State over those of another: nor shall Vessels bound to, or from, one State, be obliged to enter, clear, or pay Duties in another.

J. G. Taylor

No Money shall be drawn from the Treasury, but in Consequence of Appropriations made by Law; and a regular Statement and Account of the Receipts and Expenditures of all public Money shall be published from time to time.

No Title of Nobility shall be granted by the United States: And no Person holding any Office of Profit or Trust under them, shall, without the Consent of the Congress, accept of any present, Emolument, Office, or Title, of any kind whatever, from any King, Prince, or foreign State.

Section. 10.

No State shall enter into any Treaty, Alliance, or Confederation; grant Letters of Marque and Reprisal; coin Money; emit Bills of Credit; make any Thing but gold and silver Coin a Tender in Payment of Debts; pass any Bill of Attainder, ex post facto Law, or Law impairing the Obligation of Contracts, or grant any Title of Nobility.

No State shall, without the Consent of the Congress, lay any Imposts or Duties on Imports or Exports, except what may be absolutely necessary for executing it's inspection Laws: and the net Produce of all Duties and Imposts, laid by any State on Imports or Exports, shall be for the Use of the Treasury of the United States; and all such Laws shall be subject to the Revision and Controul of the Congress.

No State shall, without the Consent of Congress, lay any Duty of Tonnage, keep Troops, or Ships of War in time of Peace, enter into any Agreement or Compact with another State, or with a foreign Power, or engage in War, unless actually invaded, or in such imminent Danger as will not admit of delay.

J. G. Taylor

Article. II.

Section. 1.

The executive Power shall be vested in a President of the United States of America. He shall hold his Office during the Term of four Years, and, together with the Vice President, chosen for the same Term, be elected, as follows

Each State shall appoint, in such Manner as the Legislature thereof may direct, a Number of Electors, equal to the whole Number of Senators and Representatives to which the State may be entitled in the Congress: but no Senator or Representative, or Person holding an Office of Trust or Profit under the United States, shall be appointed an Elector.

The Electors shall meet in their respective States, and vote by Ballot for two Persons, of whom one at least shall not be an Inhabitant

of the same State with themselves. And they
shall make a List of all the Persons voted for,
and of the Number of Votes for each; which
List they shall sign and certify, and transmit
sealed to the Seat of the Government of the
United States, directed to the President of the
Senate. The President of the Senate shall, in
the Presence of the Senate and House of
Representatives, open all the Certificates, and
the Votes shall then be counted. The Person
having the greatest Number of Votes shall be
the President, if such Number be a Majority
of the whole Number of Electors appointed;
and if there be more than one who have such
Majority, and have an equal Number of
Votes, then the House of Representatives
shall immediately chuse by Ballot one of them
for President; and if no Person have a
Majority, then from the five highest on the
List the said House shall in like Manner
chuse the President. But in chusing the

J. G. Taylor

President, the Votes shall be taken by States, the Representation from each State having one Vote; A quorum for this Purpose shall consist of a Member or Members from two thirds of the States, and a Majority of all the States shall be necessary to a Choice. In every Case, after the Choice of the President, the Person having the greatest Number of Votes of the Electors shall be the Vice President. But if there should remain two or more who have equal Votes, the Senate shall chuse from them by Ballot the Vice President.

The Congress may determine the Time of chusing the Electors, and the Day on which they shall give their Votes; which Day shall be the same throughout the United States.

No Person except a natural born Citizen, or a Citizen of the United States, at the time of the Adoption of this Constitution, shall be eligible to the Office of President; neither shall any

Person be eligible to that Office who shall not have attained to the Age of thirty five Years, and been fourteen Years a Resident within the United States.

In Case of the Removal of the President from Office, or of his Death, Resignation, or Inability to discharge the Powers and Duties of the said Office, the Same shall devolve on the Vice President, and the Congress may by Law provide for the Case of Removal, Death, Resignation or Inability, both of the President and Vice President, declaring what Officer shall then act as President, and such Officer shall act accordingly, until the Disability be removed, or a President shall be elected.

The President shall, at stated Times, receive for his Services, a Compensation, which shall neither be encreased nor diminished during the Period for which he shall have been elected, and he shall not receive within that

J. G. Taylor

Period any other Emolument from the United States, or any of them.

Before he enter on the Execution of his Office, he shall take the following Oath or Affirmation:—"I do solemnly swear (or affirm) that I will faithfully execute the Office of President of the United States, and will to the best of my Ability, preserve, protect and defend the Constitution of the United States."

Section. 2.

The President shall be Commander in Chief of the Army and Navy of the United States, and of the Militia of the several States, when called into the actual Service of the United States; he may require the Opinion, in writing, of the principal Officer in each of the executive Departments, upon any Subject relating to the Duties of their respective Offices, and he shall have Power to grant Reprieves and Pardons for Offences against the United States, except in Cases of Impeachment.

He shall have Power, by and with the Advice and Consent of the Senate, to make Treaties, provided two thirds of the Senators present concur; and he shall nominate, and by and with the Advice and Consent of the Senate, shall appoint Ambassadors, other public Ministers and Consuls, Judges of the supreme Court, and all other Officers of the United States, whose Appointments are not herein otherwise provided for, and which shall be established by Law: but the Congress may by Law vest the Appointment of such inferior Officers, as they think proper, in the President alone, in the Courts of Law, or in the Heads of Departments.

The President shall have Power to fill up all Vacancies that may happen during the Recess of the Senate, by granting

J. G. Taylor

Commissions which shall expire at the End of their next Session.

Section. 3.

He shall from time to time give to the Congress Information of the State of the Union, and recommend to their Consideration such Measures as he shall judge necessary and expedient; he may, on extraordinary Occasions, convene both Houses, or either of them, and in Case of Disagreement between them, with Respect to the Time of Adjournment, he may adjourn them to such Time as he shall think proper; he shall receive Ambassadors and other public Ministers; he shall take Care that the Laws be faithfully executed, and shall Commission all the Officers of the United States.

Section. 4.

The President, Vice President and all civil Officers of the United States, shall be removed from Office on Impeachment for, and Conviction of, Treason, Bribery, or other high Crimes and Misdemeanors.

Article III.

Section. 1.

The judicial Power of the United States, shall be vested in one supreme Court, and in such inferior Courts as the Congress may from time to time ordain and establish. The Judges, both of the supreme and inferior Courts, shall hold their Offices during good Behaviour, and shall, at stated Times, receive for their Services, a Compensation, which shall not be diminished during their Continuance in Office.

J. G. Taylor

Section. 2.

The judicial Power shall extend to all Cases, in Law and Equity, arising under this Constitution, the Laws of the United States, and Treaties made, or which shall be made, under their Authority;—to all Cases affecting Ambassadors, other public Ministers and Consuls;—to all Cases of admiralty and maritime Jurisdiction;—to Controversies to which the United States shall be a Party;—to Controversies between two or more States;—between a State and Citizens of another State,—between Citizens of different States,—between Citizens of the same State claiming Lands under Grants of different States, and between a State, or the Citizens thereof, and foreign States, Citizens or Subjects.

In all Cases affecting Ambassadors, other public Ministers and Consuls, and those in which a State shall be Party, the supreme Court shall have original Jurisdiction. In all the other Cases before mentioned, the supreme Court shall have appellate Jurisdiction, both as to Law and Fact, with such Exceptions, and under such Regulations as the Congress shall make.

The Trial of all Crimes, except in Cases of Impeachment, shall be by Jury; and such Trial shall be held in the State where the said Crimes shall have been committed; but when not committed within any State, the Trial shall be at such Place or Places as the Congress may by Law have directed.

Section. 3.

Treason against the United States, shall consist only in levying War against them, or in adhering to their Enemies, giving them Aid and Comfort. No Person shall be convicted of Treason unless on the Testimony of two

J. G. Taylor

Witnesses to the same overt Act, or on Confession in open Court.

The Congress shall have Power to declare the Punishment of Treason, but no Attainder of Treason shall work Corruption of Blood, or Forfeiture except during the Life of the Person attainted.

Article. IV.

Section. 1.

Full Faith and Credit shall be given in each State to the public Acts, Records, and judicial Proceedings of every other State. And the Congress may by general Laws prescribe the Manner in which such Acts, Records and Proceedings shall be proved, and the Effect thereof.

Section. 2.

The Citizens of each State shall be entitled to all Privileges and Immunities of Citizens in the several States.

A Person charged in any State with Treason, Felony, or other Crime, who shall flee from Justice, and be found in another State, shall on Demand of the executive Authority of the State from which he fled, be delivered up, to be removed to the State having Jurisdiction of the Crime.

No Person held to Service or Labour in one State, under the Laws thereof, escaping into another, shall, in Consequence of any Law or Regulation therein, be discharged from such Service or Labour, but shall be delivered up on Claim of the Party to whom such Service or Labour may be due.

J. G. Taylor

Section. 3.

New States may be admitted by the Congress into this Union; but no new State shall be formed or erected within the Jurisdiction of any other State; nor any State be formed by the Junction of two or more States, or Parts of States, without the Consent of the Legislatures of the States concerned as well as of the Congress.

The Congress shall have Power to dispose of and make all needful Rules and Regulations respecting the Territory or other Property belonging to the United States; and nothing in this Constitution shall be so construed as to Prejudice any Claims of the United States, or of any particular State.

Section. 4.

The United States shall guarantee to every State in this Union a Republican Form of

Government, and shall protect each of them against Invasion; and on Application of the Legislature, or of the Executive (when the Legislature cannot be convened), against domestic Violence.

Article. V.

The Congress, whenever two thirds of both Houses shall deem it necessary, shall propose Amendments to this Constitution, or, on the Application of the Legislatures of two thirds of the several States, shall call a Convention for proposing Amendments, which, in either Case, shall be valid to all Intents and Purposes, as Part of this Constitution, when ratified by the Legislatures of three fourths of the several States, or by Conventions in three fourths thereof, as the one or the other Mode of Ratification may be proposed by the Congress; Provided that no Amendment

J. G. Taylor

which may be made prior to the Year One thousand eight hundred and eight shall in any Manner affect the first and fourth Clauses in the Ninth Section of the first Article; and that no State, without its Consent, shall be deprived of its equal Suffrage in the Senate.

Article. VI.

All Debts contracted and Engagements entered into, before the Adoption of this Constitution, shall be as valid against the United States under this Constitution, as under the Confederation.

This Constitution, and the Laws of the United States which shall be made in Pursuance thereof; and all Treaties made, or which shall be made, under the Authority of the United States, shall be the supreme Law of the Land;

and the Judges in every State shall be bound thereby, any Thing in the Constitution or Laws of any State to the Contrary notwithstanding.

The Senators and Representatives before mentioned, and the Members of the several State Legislatures, and all executive and judicial Officers, both of the United States and of the several States, shall be bound by Oath or Affirmation, to support this Constitution; but no religious Test shall ever be required as a Qualification to any Office or public Trust under the United States.

Article. VII.

The Ratification of the Conventions of nine States, shall be sufficient for the Establishment of this Constitution between the States so ratifying the Same.

J. G. Taylor

The Word, "the," being interlined between the seventh and eighth Lines of the first Page, The Word "Thirty" being partly written on an Erazure in the fifteenth Line of the first Page, The Words "is tried" being interlined between the thirty second and thirty third Lines of the first Page and the Word "the" being interlined between the forty third and forty fourth Lines of the second Page.

Attest William Jackson Secretary

done in Convention by the Unanimous Consent of the States present the Seventeenth Day of September in the Year of our Lord one thousand seven hundred and Eighty seven and of the Independance of the United States of America the Twelfth In witness whereof We have hereunto subscribed our Names,

G°. Washington
Presidt and deputy from Virginia

Delaware

Geo: Read

Gunning Bedford jun

John Dickinson

Richard Bassett

Jaco: Broom

Maryland

James McHenry

Dan of St Thos. Jenifer

Danl. Carroll

Virginia

John Blair

James Madison Jr.

North Carolina

Wm. Blount

Richd. Dobbs Spaight

Hu Williamson

J. G. Taylor

South Carolina

J. Rutledge

Charles Cotesworth Pinckney

Charles Pinckney

Pierce Butler

Georgia

William Few

Abr Baldwin

New Hampshire

John Langdon

Nicholas Gilman

Massachusetts

Nathaniel Gorham

Rufus King

Connecticut

Wm. Saml. Johnson

Roger Sherman

New York

Alexander Hamilton

New Jersey

Wil: Livingston

David Brearley

Wm. Paterson

Jona: Dayton

Pennsylvania

B Franklin

Thomas Mifflin

Robt. Morris

Geo. Clymer

Thos. FitzSimons

Jared Ingersoll

James Wilson

Gouv Morris

On September 25, 1789, the First Congress of the United States proposed 12 amendments to the Constitution. The 1789 Joint Resolution

J. G. Taylor

of Congress proposing the amendments is on display in the Rotunda in the National Archives Museum. Ten of the proposed 12 amendments were ratified by three-fourths of the state legislatures on December 15, 1791. The ratified Articles (Articles 3–12) constitute the first 10 amendments of the Constitution, or the U.S. Bill of Rights. In 1992, 203 years after it was proposed, Article 2 was ratified as the 27th Amendment to the Constitution. Article 1 was never ratified.

Transcription of the 1789 Joint Resolution of Congress Proposing 12 Amendments to the U.S. Constitution

Congress of the United States begun and held at the City of New-York, on Wednesday the fourth of March, one thousand seven hundred and eighty nine.

THE Conventions of a number of the States, having at the time of their adopting the Constitution, expressed a desire, in order to prevent misconstruction or abuse of its powers, that further declaratory and restrictive clauses should be added: And as extending the ground of public confidence in the Government, will best ensure the beneficent ends of its institution.

RESOLVED by the Senate and House of Representatives of the United States of America, in Congress assembled, two thirds of both Houses concurring, that the following Articles be proposed to the Legislatures of the several States, as amendments to the Constitution of the United States, all, or any of which Articles, when ratified by three fourths of the said Legislatures, to be valid to all intents and purposes, as part of the said Constitution; viz.

J. G. Taylor

ARTICLES in addition to, and Amendment of the Constitution of the United States of America, proposed by Congress, and ratified by the Legislatures of the several States, pursuant to the fifth Article of the original Constitution.

Article the first... After the first enumeration required by the first article of the Constitution, there shall be one Representative for every thirty thousand, until the number shall amount to one hundred, after which the proportion shall be so regulated by Congress, that there shall be not less than one hundred Representatives, nor less than one Representative for every forty thousand persons, until the number of Representatives shall amount to two hundred; after which the proportion shall be so regulated by Congress, that there shall not be less than two hundred Representatives,

nor more than one Representative for every fifty thousand persons.

Article the second... No law, varying the compensation for the services of the Senators and Representatives, shall take effect, until an election of Representatives shall have intervened.

Article the third... Congress shall make no law respecting an establishment of religion, or prohibiting the free exercise thereof; or abridging the freedom of speech, or of the press; or the right of the people peaceably to assemble, and to petition the Government for a redress of grievances.

Article the fourth... A well regulated Militia, being necessary to the security of a free State, the right of the people to keep and bear Arms, shall not be infringed.

Article the fifth... No Soldier shall, in time of peace be quartered in any house, without the

J. G. Taylor

consent of the Owner, nor in time of war, but in a manner to be prescribed by law.

Article the sixth... The right of the people to be secure in their persons, houses, papers, and effects, against unreasonable searches and seizures, shall not be violated, and no Warrants shall issue, but upon probable cause, supported by Oath or affirmation, and particularly describing the place to be searched, and the persons or things to be seized.

Article the seventh... No person shall be held to answer for a capital, or otherwise infamous crime, unless on a presentment or indictment of a Grand Jury, except in cases arising in the land or naval forces, or in the Militia, when in actual service in time of War or public danger; nor shall any person be subject for the same offence to be twice put in jeopardy of life or limb; nor shall be compelled in any criminal case to be a witness against himself, nor be deprived of life, liberty, or property, without due process of law; nor shall private property be taken for public use, without just compensation.

Article the eighth... In all criminal prosecutions, the accused shall enjoy the right to a speedy and public trial, by an impartial jury of the State and district wherein the crime shall have been committed, which district shall have been previously ascertained by law, and to be informed of the nature and cause of the accusation; to be confronted with the witnesses against him; to have compulsory process for obtaining witnesses in his favor, and to have the Assistance of Counsel for his defence.

Article the ninth... In suits at common law, where the value in controversy shall exceed twenty dollars, the right of trial by jury shall be preserved, and no fact tried by a jury,

J. G. Taylor

shall be otherwise re-examined in any Court of the United States, than according to the rules of the common law.

Article the tenth... Excessive bail shall not be required, nor excessive fines imposed, nor cruel and unusual punishments inflicted.

Article the eleventh... The enumeration in the Constitution, of certain rights, shall not be construed to deny or disparage others retained by the people.

Article the twelfth... The powers not delegated to the United States by the Constitution, nor prohibited by it to the States, are reserved to the States respectively, or to the people.

ATTEST,

Frederick Augustus Muhlenberg, Speaker of the House of Representatives
John Adams, Vice-President of the United

States, and President of the Senate
John Beckley, Clerk of the House of
Representatives.

Sam. A Otis Secretary of the Senate

The U.S. Bill of Rights

The Preamble to The Bill of Rights

Congress of the United States
begun and held at the City of New-York, on
Wednesday the fourth of March, one
thousand seven hundred and eighty nine.

THE Conventions of a number of the States,
having at the time of their adopting the
Constitution, expressed a desire, in order to
prevent misconstruction or abuse of its
powers, that further declaratory and
restrictive clauses should be added: And as
extending the ground of public confidence in
the Government, will best ensure the
beneficent ends of its institution.

J. G. Taylor

RESOLVED by the Senate and House of Representatives of the United States of America, in Congress assembled, two thirds of both Houses concurring, that the following Articles be proposed to the Legislatures of the several States, as amendments to the Constitution of the United States, all, or any of which Articles, when ratified by three fourths of the said Legislatures, to be valid to all intents and purposes, as part of the said Constitution; viz.

ARTICLES in addition to, and Amendment of the Constitution of the United States of America, proposed by Congress, and ratified by the Legislatures of the several States, pursuant to the fifth Article of the original Constitution.

Note: The following text is a transcription of the first ten amendments to the Constitution in their original form. These amendments

were ratified December 15, 1791, and form what is known as the "Bill of Rights."

Amendment I

Congress shall make no law respecting an establishment of religion, or prohibiting the free exercise thereof; or abridging the freedom of speech, or of the press; or the right of the people peaceably to assemble, and to petition the Government for a redress of grievances.

Amendment II

A well regulated Militia, being necessary to the security of a free State, the right of the people to keep and bear Arms, shall not be infringed.

Amendment III

No Soldier shall, in time of peace be quartered in any house, without the consent

J. G. Taylor

of the Owner, nor in time of war, but in a manner to be prescribed by law.

Amendment IV

The right of the people to be secure in their persons, houses, papers, and effects, against unreasonable searches and seizures, shall not be violated, and no Warrants shall issue, but upon probable cause, supported by Oath or affirmation, and particularly describing the place to be searched, and the persons or things to be seized.

Amendment V

No person shall be held to answer for a capital, or otherwise infamous crime, unless on a presentment or indictment of a Grand Jury, except in cases arising in the land or naval forces, or in the Militia, when in actual service in time of War or public danger; nor shall any person be subject for the same offence to be twice put in jeopardy of life or limb; nor shall be compelled in any criminal case to be a witness against himself, nor be deprived of life, liberty, or property, without due process of law; nor shall private property be taken for public use, without just compensation.

Amendment VI

In all criminal prosecutions, the accused shall enjoy the right to a speedy and public trial, by an impartial jury of the State and district wherein the crime shall have been committed, which district shall have been previously ascertained by law, and to be informed of the nature and cause of the accusation; to be confronted with the witnesses against him; to have compulsory process for obtaining witnesses in his favor, and to have the Assistance of Counsel for his defence.

J. G. Taylor

Amendment VII

In Suits at common law, where the value in controversy shall exceed twenty dollars, the right of trial by jury shall be preserved, and no fact tried by a jury, shall be otherwise re-examined in any Court of the United States, than according to the rules of the common law.

Amendment VIII

Excessive bail shall not be required, nor excessive fines imposed, nor cruel and unusual punishments inflicted.

Amendment IX

The enumeration in the Constitution, of certain rights, shall not be construed to deny or disparage others retained by the people.

Amendment X

The powers not delegated to the United States by the Constitution, nor prohibited by it to the States, are reserved to the States respectively, or to the people.

MENDMENT XI

Passed by Congress March 4, 1794. Ratified February 7, 1795.

Note: Article III, section 2, of the Constitution was modified by amendment 11. The Judicial power of the United States shall not be construed to extend to any suit in law or equity, commenced or prosecuted against one of the United States by Citizens of another State, or by Citizens or Subjects of any Foreign State.

AMENDMENT XII

Passed by Congress December 9, 1803. Ratified June 15, 1804.

J. G. Taylor

Note: A portion of Article II, section 1 of the Constitution was superseded by the 12th amendment. The Electors shall meet in their respective states and vote by ballot for President and Vice-President, one of whom, at least, shall not be an inhabitant of the same state with themselves; they shall name in their ballots the person voted for as President, and in distinct ballots the person voted for as Vice-President, and they shall make distinct lists of all persons voted for as President, and of all persons voted for as Vice-President, and of the number of votes for each, which lists they shall sign and certify, and transmit sealed to the seat of the government of the United States, directed to the President of the Senate; -- the President of the Senate shall, in the presence of the Senate and House of Representatives, open all the certificates and the votes shall then be counted; -- The person having the greatest number of votes for President, shall be the President, if such number be a majority of the whole number of Electors appointed; and if no person have such majority, then from the persons having the highest numbers not exceeding three on the list of those voted for as President, the House of Representatives shall choose immediately, by ballot, the President. But in choosing the President, the votes shall be taken by states, the representation from each state having one vote; a quorum for this purpose shall consist of a member or members from two-thirds of the states, and a majority of all the states shall be necessary to a choice. [And if the House of Representatives shall not choose a President whenever the right of choice shall devolve upon them, before the fourth day of March next following, then the Vice-President shall act as President, as in case of the death or other constitutional disability of

J. G. Taylor

the President. --]* The person having the greatest number of votes as Vice-President, shall be the Vice-President, if such number be a majority of the whole number of Electors appointed, and if no person have a majority, then from the two highest numbers on the list, the Senate shall choose the Vice-President; a quorum for the purpose shall consist of two-thirds of the whole number of Senators, and a majority of the whole number shall be necessary to a choice. But no person constitutionally ineligible to the office of President shall be eligible to that of Vice-President of the United States. *Superseded by section 3 of the 20th amendment.

AMENDMENT XIII

Passed by Congress January 31, 1865.
Ratified December 6, 1865.

Note: A portion of Article IV, section 2, of the Constitution was superseded by the 13th amendment.

Section 1.

Neither slavery nor involuntary servitude, except as a punishment for crime whereof the party shall have been duly convicted, shall exist within the United States, or any place subject to their jurisdiction.

Section 2.

Congress shall have power to enforce this article by appropriate legislation.

AMENDMENT XIV

Passed by Congress June 13, 1866. Ratified July 9, 1868.

J. G. Taylor

Note: Article I, section 2, of the Constitution was modified by section 2 of the 14th amendment.

Section 1.

All persons born or naturalized in the United States, and subject to the jurisdiction thereof, are citizens of the United States and of the State wherein they reside. No State shall make or enforce any law which shall abridge the privileges or immunities of citizens of the United States; nor shall any State deprive any person of life, liberty, or property, without due process of law; nor deny to any person within its jurisdiction the equal protection of the laws.

Section 2.

Representatives shall be apportioned among the several States according to their respective numbers, counting the whole number of persons in each State, excluding Indians not taxed. But when the right to vote at any election for the choice of electors for President and Vice-President of the United States, Representatives in Congress, the Executive and Judicial officers of a State, or the members of the Legislature thereof, is denied to any of the male inhabitants of such State, being twenty-one years of age,* and citizens of the United States, or in any way abridged, except for participation in rebellion, or other crime, the basis of representation therein shall be reduced in the proportion which the number of such male citizens shall bear to the whole number of male citizens twenty-one years of age in such State.

Section 3.

No person shall be a Senator or Representative in Congress, or elector of

J. G. Taylor

President and Vice-President, or hold any office, civil or military, under the United States, or under any State, who, having previously taken an oath, as a member of Congress, or as an officer of the United States, or as a member of any State legislature, or as an executive or judicial officer of any State, to support the Constitution of the United States, shall have engaged in insurrection or rebellion against the same, or given aid or comfort to the enemies thereof. But Congress may by a vote of two-thirds of each House, remove such disability.

Section 4.

The validity of the public debt of the United States, authorized by law, including debts incurred for payment of pensions and bounties for services in suppressing insurrection or rebellion, shall not be questioned. But neither the United States nor any State shall assume or pay any debt or obligation incurred in aid of insurrection or rebellion against the United States, or any claim for the loss or emancipation of any slave; but all such debts, obligations and claims shall be held illegal and void.

Section 5.

The Congress shall have the power to enforce, by appropriate legislation, the provisions of this article.

*Changed by section 1 of the 26th amendment.

AMENDMENT XV

Passed by Congress February 26, 1869. Ratified February 3, 1870.

J. G. Taylor

Section 1.

The right of citizens of the United States to vote shall not be denied or abridged by the United States or by any State on account of race, color, or previous condition of servitude--

Section 2.

The Congress shall have the power to enforce this article by appropriate legislation.

AMENDMENT XVI

Passed by Congress July 2, 1909. Ratified February 3, 1913.

Note: Article I, section 9, of the Constitution was modified by amendment 16.

The Congress shall have power to lay and collect taxes on incomes, from whatever source derived, without apportionment

among the several States, and without regard to any census or enumeration.

AMENDMENT XVII

Passed by Congress May 13, 1912. Ratified April 8, 1913.

Note: Article I, section 3, of the Constitution was modified by the 17th amendment.

The Senate of the United States shall be composed of two Senators from each State, elected by the people thereof, for six years; and each Senator shall have one vote. The electors in each State shall have the qualifications requisite for electors of the most numerous branch of the State legislatures.

When vacancies happen in the representation of any State in the Senate, the executive authority of such State shall issue writs of

J. G. Taylor

election to fill such vacancies: Provided, That the legislature of any State may empower the executive thereof to make temporary appointments until the people fill the vacancies by election as the legislature may direct.

This amendment shall not be so construed as to affect the election or term of any Senator chosen before it becomes valid as part of the Constitution.

AMENDMENT XVIII

Passed by Congress December 18, 1917. Ratified January 16, 1919. Repealed by amendment 21.

Section 1.

After one year from the ratification of this article the manufacture, sale, or transportation of intoxicating liquors within, the importation thereof into, or the exportation thereof from the United States and all territory subject to the jurisdiction thereof for beverage purposes is hereby prohibited.

Section 2.

The Congress and the several States shall have concurrent power to enforce this article by appropriate legislation.

Section 3.

This article shall be inoperative unless it shall have been ratified as an amendment to the Constitution by the legislatures of the several States, as provided in the Constitution, within seven years from the date of the submission hereof to the States by the Congress.

J. G. Taylor

AMENDMENT XIX

Passed by Congress June 4, 1919. Ratified August 18, 1920.

The right of citizens of the United States to vote shall not be denied or abridged by the United States or by any State on account of sex.

Congress shall have power to enforce this article by appropriate legislation.

AMENDMENT XX

Passed by Congress March 2, 1932. Ratified January 23, 1933.

Note: Article I, section 4, of the Constitution was modified by section 2 of this amendment. In addition, a portion of the 12th amendment was superseded by section 3.

Section 1.

The terms of the President and the Vice President shall end at noon on the 20th day of January, and the terms of Senators and Representatives at noon on the 3d day of January, of the years in which such terms would have ended if this article had not been ratified; and the terms of their successors shall then begin.

Section 2.

The Congress shall assemble at least once in every year, and such meeting shall begin at noon on the 3d day of January, unless they shall by law appoint a different day.

Section 3.

If, at the time fixed for the beginning of the term of the President, the President elect shall have died, the Vice President elect shall become President. If a President shall not

J. G. Taylor

have been chosen before the time fixed for the beginning of his term, or if the President elect shall have failed to qualify, then the Vice President elect shall act as President until a President shall have qualified; and the Congress may by law provide for the case wherein neither a President elect nor a Vice President elect shall have qualified, declaring who shall then act as President, or the manner in which one who is to act shall be selected, and such person shall act accordingly until a President or Vice President shall have qualified.

Section 4.

The Congress may by law provide for the case of the death of any of the persons from whom the House of Representatives may choose a President whenever the right of choice shall have devolved upon them, and for the case of the death of any of the persons from whom the Senate may choose a Vice President whenever the right of choice shall have devolved upon them.

Section 5.

Sections 1 and 2 shall take effect on the 15th day of October following the ratification of this article.

Section 6.

This article shall be inoperative unless it shall have been ratified as an amendment to the Constitution by the legislatures of three-fourths of the several States within seven years from the date of its submission.

AMENDMENT XXI

Passed by Congress February 20, 1933.
Ratified December 5, 1933.

J. G. Taylor

Section 1.

The eighteenth article of amendment to the Constitution of the United States is hereby repealed.

Section 2.

The transportation or importation into any State, Territory, or possession of the United States for delivery or use therein of intoxicating liquors, in violation of the laws thereof, is hereby prohibited.

Section 3.

This article shall be inoperative unless it shall have been ratified as an amendment to the Constitution by conventions in the several States, as provided in the Constitution, within seven years from the date of the submission hereof to the States by the Congress.

AMENDMENT XXII

Passed by Congress March 21, 1947. Ratified February 27, 1951.

Section 1.

No person shall be elected to the office of the President more than twice, and no person who has held the office of President, or acted as President, for more than two years of a term to which some other person was elected President shall be elected to the office of the President more than once. But this Article shall not apply to any person holding the office of President when this Article was proposed by the Congress, and shall not prevent any person who may be holding the office of President, or acting as President, during the term within which this Article becomes operative from holding the office of President or acting as President during the remainder of such term.

J. G. Taylor

Section 2.

This article shall be inoperative unless it shall have been ratified as an amendment to the Constitution by the legislatures of three-fourths of the several States within seven years from the date of its submission to the States by the Congress.

AMENDMENT XXIII

Passed by Congress June 16, 1960. Ratified March 29, 1961.

Section 1.

The District constituting the seat of Government of the United States shall appoint in such manner as the Congress may direct:

A number of electors of President and Vice President equal to the whole number of

Senators and Representatives in Congress to
which the District would be entitled if it were
a State, but in no event more than the least
populous State; they shall be in addition to
those appointed by the States, but they shall
be considered, for the purposes of the election
of President and Vice President, to be
electors appointed by a State; and they shall
meet in the District and perform such duties
as provided by the twelfth article of
amendment.

Section 2.

The Congress shall have power to enforce
this article by appropriate legislation.

AMENDMENT XXIV

Passed by Congress August 27, 1962. Ratified
January 23, 1964.

J. G. Taylor

Section 1.

The right of citizens of the United States to vote in any primary or other election for President or Vice President, for electors for President or Vice President, or for Senator or Representative in Congress, shall not be denied or abridged by the United States or any State by reason of failure to pay any poll tax or other tax.

Section 2.

The Congress shall have power to enforce this article by appropriate legislation.

AMENDMENT XXV

Passed by Congress July 6, 1965. Ratified February 10, 1967.

Note: Article II, section 1, of the Constitution was affected by the 25th amendment.

Section 1.

In case of the removal of the President from office or of his death or resignation, the Vice President shall become President.

Section 2.

Whenever there is a vacancy in the office of the Vice President, the President shall nominate a Vice President who shall take office upon confirmation by a majority vote of both Houses of Congress.

Section 3.

Whenever the President transmits to the President pro tempore of the Senate and the Speaker of the House of Representatives his written declaration that he is unable to discharge the powers and duties of his office, and until he transmits to them a written declaration to the contrary, such powers and

J. G. Taylor

duties shall be discharged by the Vice President as Acting President.

Section 4.

Whenever the Vice President and a majority of either the principal officers of the executive departments or of such other body as Congress may by law provide, transmit to the President pro tempore of the Senate and the Speaker of the House of Representatives their written declaration that the President is unable to discharge the powers and duties of his office, the Vice President shall immediately assume the powers and duties of the office as Acting President.

Thereafter, when the President transmits to the President pro tempore of the Senate and the Speaker of the House of Representatives his written declaration that no inability exists, he shall resume the powers and duties of his office unless the Vice President and a majority of either the principal officers of the executive department or of such other body as Congress may by law provide, transmit within four days to the President pro tempore of the Senate and the Speaker of the House of Representatives their written declaration that the President is unable to discharge the powers and duties of his office. Thereupon Congress shall decide the issue, assembling within forty-eight hours for that purpose if not in session. If the Congress, within twenty-one days after receipt of the latter written declaration, or, if Congress is not in session, within twenty-one days after Congress is required to assemble, determines by two-thirds vote of both Houses that the President is unable to discharge the powers and duties of his office, the Vice President shall continue to discharge the same as Acting President; otherwise, the President shall resume the powers and duties of his office.

AMENDMENT XXVI

Passed by Congress March 23, 1971. Ratified July 1, 1971.

Note: Amendment 14, section 2, of the Constitution was modified by section 1 of the 26th amendment.

Section 1.

The right of citizens of the United States, who are eighteen years of age or older, to vote shall not be denied or abridged by the United States or by any State on account of age.

Section 2.

The Congress shall have power to enforce this article by appropriate legislation.

AMENDMENT XXVII

Originally proposed Sept. 25, 1789. Ratified May 7, 1992.

No law, varying the compensation for the services of the Senators and Representatives, shall take effect, until an election of Representatives shall have intervened.

Chapter 6

Checks and Balances

My greatest hope is that you have just read the entire Constitution of the United States of America. On each reading I am inspired by the great men and woman who brought this great country to reality.

J. G. Taylor

My fear in the face of all the happenings in our world is that the vision of our great and forward thinking forbearers has not and will not be lost to us as a people or to the person whom I have dedicated this book the one lone voter.

You in your voting booth decide for yourself for whom and how you will vote.

You have the voice.

You have the power.

The checks and balances of United States government are the three branches of this government.

The full name of the republic is "United States of America". No other name appears in the Constitution, and this is the name that appears on money, in treaties, and in legal cases to which it is a party (e.g. Charles T. Schenck v. United States). The terms "Government of the United States of America" or "United States Government" are often used in official documents to represent the federal government as distinct from the states collectively. In casual conversation or writing, the term "Federal Government" is often used, and the term "National Government" is sometimes used.

The terms "Federal" and "National" in government agency or program names generally indicate affiliation with the federal government (e.g. Federal Bureau of Investigation, National Oceanic and Atmospheric Administration, etc.). Because the seat of government is in Washington, D.C., "Washington" is commonly used as a metonym for the federal government.

J. G. Taylor

History

The outline of the government of the United States is laid out in the Constitution. The government was formed in 1789, making the United States one of the world's first, if not the first, modern national constitutional republics.[1]

The United States government is based on the principles of federalism and republicanism, in which power is shared between the federal government and state governments. The interpretation and execution of these principles, including what powers the federal government should have and how those powers can be exercised, have been debated ever since the adoption of the Constitution.

Some make the case for expansive federal powers while others argue for a more limited role for the central government in relation to individuals, the states or other recognized entities.

Since the American Civil War, the powers of the federal government have generally expanded greatly, although there have been periods since that time of legislative branch dominance (e.g., the decades immediately following the Civil War) or when states' rights proponents have succeeded in limiting federal power through legislative action, executive prerogative or by constitutional interpretation by the courts.[2][3]

One of the theoretical pillars of the United States Constitution is the idea of "checks and balances" among the powers and responsibilities of the three branches of American government: the executive, the legislative and the judiciary. For example, while the legislative (Congress) has the power

J. G. Taylor

to create law, the executive (President) can veto any legislation—an act which, in turn, can be overridden by Congress.[4] The President nominates judges to the nation's highest judiciary authority (Supreme Court), but those nominees must be approved by Congress. The Supreme Court, in its turn, has the power to invalidate as "unconstitutional" any law passed by the Congress. These and other examples are examined in more detail in the text below.

Legislative branch

Main article: United States Congress

Seal of the U.S. Congress

The United States Congress is the legislative branch of the federal government. It is bicameral, comprising the House of Representatives and the Senate.

Makeup of Congress

House of Representatives

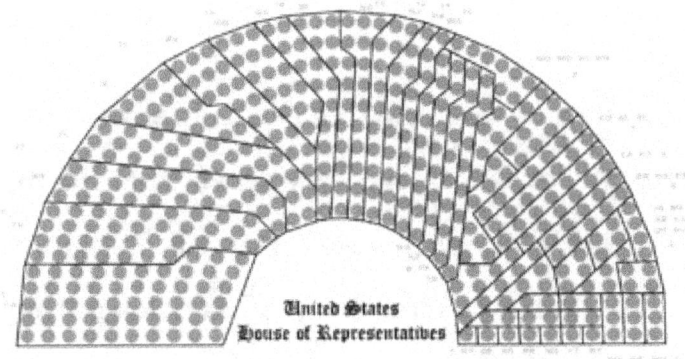

The 435 seats of the House grouped by state

The House currently consists of 435 voting members, each of whom represents a congressional district. The number of representatives each state has in the House is based on each state's population as

J. G. Taylor

determined in the most recent United States Census. All 435 representatives serve a two-year term. Each state receives a minimum of one representative in the House. In order to be elected as a representative, an individual must be at least 25 years of age, must have been a U.S. citizen for at least seven years, and must live in the state that he or she represents.

There is no limit on the number of terms a representative may serve. In addition to the 435 voting members, there are six non-voting members, consisting of five delegates and one resident commissioner. There is one delegate each from the District of Columbia, Guam, the Virgin Islands, American Samoa and the Commonwealth of the Northern Mariana Islands, and the resident commissioner from Puerto Rico.[5]

Senate

In contrast, the Senate is made up of two senators from each state, regardless of population. There are currently 100 senators (two from each of the 50 states), who each serve six-year terms. Approximately one third of the Senate stands for election every two years.

Different powers

The House and Senate each have particular exclusive powers. For example, the Senate must approve (give "advice and consent" to) many important Presidential appointments, including cabinet officers, federal judges (including nominees to the Supreme Court), department secretaries (heads of federal executive branch departments), U.S. military and naval officers, and ambassadors to foreign countries. All legislative bills for raising

J. G. Taylor

revenue must originate in the House of
Representatives. The approval of both
chambers is required to pass any legislation,
which then may only become law by being
signed by the President (or, if the President
vetoes the bill, both houses of Congress then
re-pass the bill, but by a two-thirds majority
of each chamber, in which case the bill
becomes law without the President's
signature).

The powers of Congress are limited to
those enumerated in the Constitution; all
other powers are reserved to the states and
the people. The Constitution also includes the
"Necessary and Proper Clause", which
grants Congress the power to "make all laws
which shall be necessary and proper for
carrying into execution the foregoing
powers". Members of the House and Senate
are elected by first-past-the-post voting in

every state except Louisiana, and Georgia, which have runoffs.

Impeachment of federal officers

Congress has the power to remove the President, federal judges, and other federal officers from office. The House of Representatives and Senate have separate roles in this process. The House must first vote to "impeach" the official. Then, a trial is held in the Senate to decide whether the official should be removed from office. Although two presidents have been impeached by the House of Representatives (Andrew Johnson and Bill Clinton), neither of them was removed following trial in the Senate.

Congressional procedures

Article I, Section 2, paragraph 2 of the U.S. Constitution gives each chamber the

J. G. Taylor

power to "determine the rules of its proceedings". From this provision were created congressional committees, which do the work of drafting legislation and conducting congressional investigations into national matters. The 108th Congress (2003–2005) had 19 standing committees in the House and 17 in the Senate, plus four joint permanent committees with members from both houses overseeing the Library of Congress, printing, taxation and the economy. In addition, each house may name special, or select, committees to study specific problems. Today, much of the congressional workload is borne by subcommittees, of which there are some 150.

Powers of Congress

Main article: Article One of the United States Constitution

The United States Capitol is the seat of government for Congress.

The Constitution grants numerous powers to Congress. Enumerated in Article I, Section 8, these include the powers to levy and collect taxes; to coin money and regulate its value; provide for punishment for counterfeiting; establish post offices and roads, issue patents, create federal courts inferior to the Supreme Court, combat piracies and felonies, declare war, raise and support armies, provide and maintain a navy, make rules for the regulation of land and naval forces, provide for, arm and discipline the militia, exercise exclusive legislation in the District of Columbia, and to make laws necessary to properly execute powers.

J. G. Taylor

Over the two centuries since the United States was formed, many disputes have arisen over the limits on the powers of the federal government. These disputes have often been the subject of lawsuits that have ultimately been decided by the United States Supreme Court.

Congressional oversight

Main article: Congressional oversight

Congressional oversight is intended to prevent waste and fraud, protect civil liberties and individual rights, ensure executive compliance with the law, gather information for making laws and educating the public, and evaluate executive performance.[6]

It applies to cabinet departments, executive agencies, regulatory commissions and the presidency.

Congress's oversight function takes many forms:

- **Committee inquiries and hearings**
- **Formal consultations with and reports from the President**
- **Senate advice and consent for presidential nominations and for treaties**
- **House impeachment proceedings and subsequent Senate trials**
- **House and Senate proceedings under the 25th Amendment in the event that the President becomes disabled or the office of the Vice President falls vacant.**
- **Informal meetings between legislators and executive officials**
- **Congressional membership: each state is allocated a number of seats based on its representation (or ostensible representation, in the case of D.C.) in the House of Representatives. Each**

J. G. Taylor

state is allocated two Senators regardless of its population. As of January 2010, the District of Columbia elects a non-voting representative to the House of Representatives along with American Samoa, the U.S. Virgin Islands, Guam, Puerto Rico and the Northern Mariana Islands.

Executive branch

See also: Article Two of the United States Constitution and United States Executive Orders

The executive power in the federal government is vested in the President of the United States,[7] although power is often delegated to the Cabinet members and other officials.[8][9] The President and Vice President are elected as running mates by the Electoral College, for which each state, as well as the District of Columbia, is allocated a number of seats based on its representation (or ostensible representation, in the case of D.C.) in both houses of Congress.[7][10]

The President is limited to a maximum of two four-year terms.[11] If the President has already served two years or more of a term to which some other person was elected, he may only serve one more additional four-year term.

President

Seal of the U.S. President

J. G. Taylor

The executive branch consists of the President and those to whom the President's powers are delegated. The President is both the head of state and government, as well as the military commander-in-chief and chief diplomat. The President, according to the Constitution, must "take care that the laws be faithfully executed", and "preserve, protect and defend the Constitution". The President presides over the executive branch of the federal government, an organization numbering about 5 million people, including 1 million active-duty military personnel and 600,000 postal service employees.

The President may sign legislation passed by Congress into law or may veto it, preventing it from becoming law unless two-thirds of both houses of Congress vote to override the veto. The President may unilaterally sign treaties with foreign nations.

However, ratification of international treaties requires a two-thirds majority vote in the Senate. The President may be impeached by a majority in the House and removed from office by a two-thirds majority in the Senate for "treason, bribery, or other high crimes and misdemeanors".

The President may not dissolve Congress or call special elections but does have the power to pardon, or release, criminals convicted of offenses against the federal government (except in cases of impeachment), enact executive orders, and (with the consent of the Senate) appoint Supreme Court justices and federal judges.

Vice President

J. G. Taylor

Seal of the U.S. Vice President

The Vice President is the second-highest official in rank of the federal government. The office of the Vice President's duties and powers are established in the legislative branch of the federal government under Article 1, Section 3, Clauses 4 and 5 as the President of the Senate. By virtue of this on-going role, he or she is the head of the Senate. In that capacity, the Vice President is allowed to vote in the Senate, but only when necessary to break a tie vote. Pursuant to the Twelfth Amendment, the Vice President presides over

the joint session of Congress when it convenes to count the vote of the Electoral College.

As first in the U.S. presidential line of succession, the Vice President duties and powers move to the executive branch when becoming President upon the death, resignation, or removal of the President, which has happened nine times in U.S. history. Lastly, in the case of a Twenty-fifth Amendment succession event, Vice President would become Acting President, assuming all of the powers and duties of President, except being designated as President. Accordingly, by circumstances, the Constitution designates the Vice President as routinely in the legislative branch, or succeeding to the executive branch as President, or possibly being in both as Acting President pursuant to the Twenty-fifth Amendment. Because of circumstances, the overlapping nature of the duties and powers attributed to the office, the

J. G. Taylor

title of the office and other matters, such has generated a spirited scholarly dispute regarding attaching an exclusive branch designation to the office of Vice President.[12][13]

Cabinet, executive departments, and agencies

The day-to-day enforcement and administration of federal laws is in the hands of the various federal executive departments, created by Congress to deal with specific areas of national and international affairs.

The heads of the 15 departments, chosen by the President and approved with the "advice and consent" of the U.S. Senate, form a council of advisers generally known as the President's "Cabinet". In addition to departments, a number of staff organizations are grouped into the Executive Office of the President.

These include the White House staff, the National Security Council, the Office of Management and Budget, the Council of Economic Advisers, the Council on Environmental Quality, the Office of the U.S. Trade Representative, the Office of National Drug Control Policy and the Office of Science and Technology Policy. The employees in these United States government agencies are called federal civil servants.

There are also independent agencies such as the United States Postal Service, the National Aeronautics and Space Administration (NASA), the Central Intelligence Agency (CIA), the Environmental Protection Agency, and the United States Agency for International Development. In addition, there are government-owned corporations such as the

148

J. G. Taylor

Federal Deposit Insurance Corporation and the National Railroad Passenger Corporation.

Judicial branch

The Judiciary explains and applies the laws. This branch does this by hearing and eventually making decisions on various legal cases.

Overview of the federal judiciary

Seal of the U.S. Supreme Court

Article III section I of the Constitution establishes the Supreme Court of the United States and authorizes the United States Congress to establish inferior (i.e., lower) courts as their need shall arise. Section I also establishes a lifetime tenure for all federal judges and states that their compensation may not be diminished during their time in office. Article II section II establishes that all federal judges are to be appointed by the president and confirmed by the United States Senate.

The Judiciary Act of 1789 subdivided the nation jurisdictionally into judicial districts and created federal courts for each district. The three tiered structure of this act established the basic structure of the national judiciary: the Supreme Court, 13 courts of appeals, 94 district courts, and two courts of special jurisdiction. Congress retains the

J. G. Taylor

power to re-organize or even abolish federal courts lower than the Supreme Court.

The U.S. Supreme Court adjudicates "cases and controversies"—matters pertaining to the federal government, disputes between states, and interpretation of the United States Constitution, and, in general, can declare legislation or executive action made at any level of the government as unconstitutional, nullifying the law and creating precedent for future law and decisions. The United States Constitution does not specifically mention the power of judicial review (the power to declare a law unconstitutional). The power of judicial review was asserted by Chief Justice Marshall in the landmark Supreme Court Case Marbury v. Madison (1803).

There have been instances in the past where such declarations have been ignored by the other two branches. Below the U.S. Supreme Court are the United States Courts of Appeals, and below them in turn are the United States District Courts, which are the general trial courts for federal law, and for certain controversies between litigants who are not deemed citizens of the same state ("diversity jurisdiction").

There are three levels of federal courts with general jurisdiction, meaning that these courts handle criminal cases and civil lawsuits between individuals. Other courts, such as the bankruptcy courts and the Tax Court, are specialized courts handling only certain kinds of cases ("subject matter jurisdiction").

The Bankruptcy Courts are "under" the supervision of the district courts, and, as such, are not considered part of the "Article III" judiciary and also as such their judges

J. G. Taylor

do not have lifetime tenure, nor are they
Constitutionally exempt from diminution of
their remuneration.[14]

Also the Tax Court is not an Article III
court (but is, instead an "Article I Court").[15]

The district courts are the trial courts
wherein cases that are considered under the
Judicial Code (Title 28, United States Code)
consistent with the jurisdictional precepts of
"federal question jurisdiction" and
"diversity jurisdiction" and "pendent
jurisdiction" can be filed and decided. The
district courts can also hear cases under
"removal jurisdiction", wherein a case
brought in State court meets the
requirements for diversity jurisdiction, and
one party litigant chooses to "remove" the
case from state court to federal court.

The United States Courts of Appeals are appellate courts that hear appeals of cases decided by the district courts, and some direct appeals from administrative agencies, and some interlocutory appeals. The U.S. Supreme Court hears appeals from the decisions of the courts of appeals or state supreme courts, and in addition has original jurisdiction over a few cases.

The judicial power extends to cases arising under the Constitution, an Act of Congress; a U.S. treaty; cases affecting ambassadors, ministers and consuls of foreign countries in the U.S.; cases and controversies to which the federal government is a party; controversies between states (or their citizens) and foreign nations (or their citizens or subjects); and bankruptcy cases (collectively "federal-question jurisdiction").

J. G. Taylor

The Eleventh Amendment removed from federal jurisdiction cases in which citizens of one state were the plaintiffs and the government of another state was the defendant. It did not disturb federal jurisdiction in cases in which a state government is a plaintiff and a citizen of another state the defendant.

The power of the federal courts extends both to civil actions for damages and other redress, and to criminal cases arising under federal law. The interplay of the Supremacy Clause and Article III has resulted in a complex set of relationships between state and federal courts. Federal courts can sometimes hear cases arising under state law pursuant to diversity jurisdiction, state courts can decide certain matters involving federal law, and a handful of federal claims are primarily reserved by federal statute to the state courts (for example, those arising from the Telephone Consumer Protection Act of 1991).

Both court systems thus can be said to have exclusive jurisdiction in some areas and concurrent jurisdiction in others.

The U.S. Constitution safeguards judicial independence by providing that federal judges shall hold office "during good behavior"; in practice, this usually means they serve until they die, retire, or resign. A judge who commits an offense while in office may be impeached in the same way as the President or other officials of the federal government. U.S. judges are appointed by the President, subject to confirmation by the Senate. Another Constitutional provision prohibits Congress from reducing the pay of any Article III judge (Congress is able to set a lower salary for all future judges that take

J. G. Taylor

office after the reduction, but may not decrease the rate of pay for judges already in office).

Relationships between state and federal courts

Separate from, but not entirely independent of, this federal court system are the court systems of each state, each dealing with, in addition to federal law when not deemed preempted, a state's own laws, and having its own court rules and procedures. Although state governments and the federal government are legally dual sovereigns, the Supreme Court of the United States is in many cases the appellate court from the State Supreme Courts (e.g., absent the Court countenancing the applicability of the doctrine of adequate and independent State grounds). The Supreme Courts of each state are by this doctrine the final authority on the interpretation of the applicable state's laws and Constitution.

Many state constitution provisions are equal in breadth to those of the U.S. Constitution, but are considered "parallel" (thus, where, for example, the right to privacy pursuant to a state constitution is broader than the federal right to privacy, and the asserted ground is explicitly held to be "independent", the question can be finally decided in a State Supreme Court—the U.S. Supreme Court will decline to take jurisdiction).

A State Supreme Court, other than of its own accord, is bound only by the U.S. Supreme Court's interpretation of federal law, but is not bound by interpretation of federal law by the federal court of appeals for the federal circuit in which the state is included, or even the federal district courts

J. G. Taylor

located in the state, a result of the dual sovereigns concept.

Conversely, a federal district court hearing a matter involving only a question of state law (usually through diversity jurisdiction) must apply the substantive law of the state in which the court sits, a result of the application of the <u>Erie Doctrine</u>; however, at the same time, the case is heard under the Federal Rules of Civil Procedure, the Federal Rules of Criminal Procedure and the Federal Rules of Evidence instead of state procedural rules (that is, the application of the Erie Doctrine only extends to a requirement that a federal court asserting diversity jurisdiction apply substantive state law, but not procedural state law, which may be different). Together, the laws of the federal and state governments form U.S. law.

Elections and voting

Main article: Elections in the United States

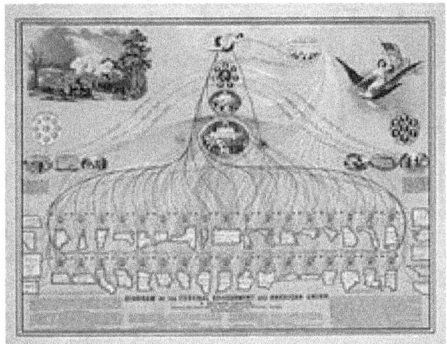

Diagram of the Federal Government and American Union, 1862.

Suffrage, commonly known as the ability to vote, has changed significantly over time. In the early years of the United States, voting was considered a matter for state governments, and was commonly restricted to white men who owned land. Direct elections were mostly held only for the U.S. House of Representatives and state legislatures, although what specific bodies were elected by the electorate varied from state to state.

J. G. Taylor

Under this original system, both senators representing each state in the U.S. Senate were chosen by a majority vote of the state legislature. Since the ratification of the Seventeenth Amendment in 1913, members of both houses of Congress have been directly elected. Today, U.S. citizens have almost universal suffrage under equal protection of the laws[16] from the age of 18,[17] regardless of race,[18] gender,[19] or wealth.[20] The only significant exception to this is the disenfranchisement of convicted felons, and in some states former felons as well.

Under the U.S. Constitution, the national representation of U.S. territories and the federal district of Washington, D.C. in Congress is limited: while residents of the District of Columbia are subject to federal laws and federal taxes, their only congressional representative is a non-voting delegate; however, they have been allowed to participate in presidential elections since March 29, 1961.[21]

Residents of U.S. territories have varying rights; for example, only some residents of Puerto Rico pay federal income taxes (though all residents must pay all other federal taxes, including import/export taxes, federal commodity taxes and federal payroll taxes, including Social Security and Medicare).

All federal laws that are "not locally inapplicable" are automatically the law of the land in Puerto Rico but their current representation in the U.S. Congress is in the form of a Resident Commissioner, a nonvoting delegate.[22]

State, tribal, and local governments
Main articles: State governments of the United States, Tribal sovereignty in the

J. G. Taylor

United States, and Local government in the United States

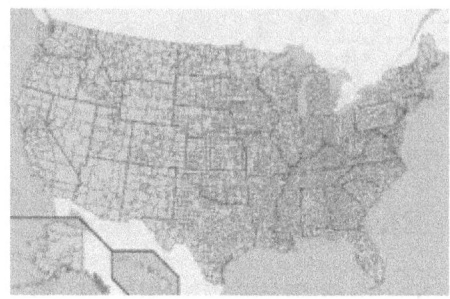

The states of the United States as divided into <u>counties</u> (or, in Louisiana and Alaska, parishes and boroughs, respectively). Alaska and Hawaii are not to scale and the Aleutian and uninhabited Northwestern Hawaiian Islands have been omitted.

The state governments tend to have the greatest influence over most Americans' daily lives. The Tenth Amendment prohibits the federal government from exercising any power not delegated to it by the States in the Constitution; as a result, states handle the majority of issues most relevant to individuals within their jurisdiction.

Because state governments are not authorized to print currency, they generally have to raise revenue through either taxes or bonds. As a result, state governments tend to impose severe budget cuts or raise taxes any time the economy is faltering.[23]

Each state has its own written constitution, government and code of laws. The Constitution stipulates only that each state must have, "a Republican Government". Therefore, there are often great differences in law and procedure between individual states, concerning issues such as property, crime, health and education, amongst others. The highest elected official of each state is the Governor. Each state also has an elected state legislature (bicameralism is a feature of every state except Nebraska), whose members represent the voters of the state.

J. G. Taylor

Each state maintains its own state court system. In some states, supreme and lower court justices are elected by the people; in others, they are appointed, as they are in the federal system.

As a result of the Supreme Court case Worcester v. Georgia, American Indian tribes are considered "domestic dependent nations" that operate as sovereign governments subject to federal authority but, in some cases, outside of the jurisdiction of state governments.

Hundreds of laws, executive orders and court cases have modified the governmental status of tribes vis-à-vis individual states, but the two have continued to be recognized as separate bodies. Tribal governments vary in robustness, from a simple council used to manage all aspects of tribal affairs, to large and complex bureaucracies with several branches of government.

Tribes are currently encouraged to form their own governments, with power resting in elected tribal councils, elected tribal chairpersons, or religiously appointed leaders (as is the case with pueblos). Tribal citizenship and voting rights are typically restricted to individuals of native descent, but tribes are free to set whatever citizenship requirements they wish.

The institutions that are responsible for local government within states are typically town, city, or county boards, water management districts, fire management districts, library districts and other similar governmental units which make laws that affect their particular area. These laws concern issues such as traffic, the sale of alcohol and the keeping of animals.

J. G. Taylor

The highest elected official of a town or city is usually the mayor. In New England, towns operate in a direct democratic fashion, and in some states, such as Rhode Island, Connecticut, and some parts of Massachusetts, counties have little or no power, existing only as geographic distinctions.

In other areas, county governments have more power, such as to collect taxes and maintain law enforcement agencies.

Source: Wikipedia

Chapter 8

So what now?

Writing and compiling this book I am exercising my right of Freedom of Speech as given to me by the First Amendment included herein.

Further Section 4 of the 25th Amendment tells it all. If you haven't read it go back this section.

The Presidency of the United States of America is not about one man. The Presidency is bigger than any individual. It's the way it was set up in the beginning and it's the way it works.

The checks and balances of each branch of our government make it possible to

J. G. Taylor

keep the other from stepping over it bounds if one should be found to be stepping over then the other two must come forward and stop it from happening.

There are no levels of freedom in the United States of America. As citizens of the United States of American freedom is one of your most valued possessions. Do not take it lightly.

Again I'm not saying we should use the 25th Amendment and I'm not saying we shouldn't use it, I'm saying we need to look at it as a choice. Because we are a free people who have the Freedom of Choice.

Thank you for your time.